Summer Music

FOR FLUTE AND PIANO   Richard Rodney Bennett

GRADE VII

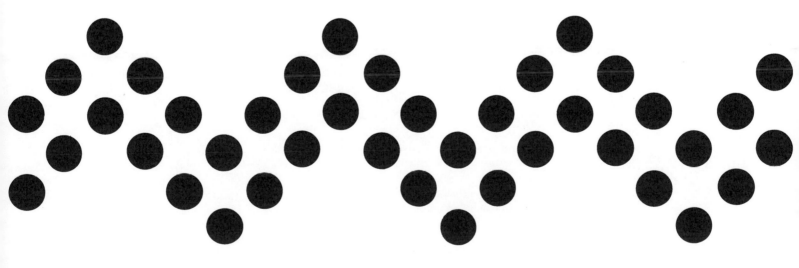

Order No: NOV 120560

NOVELLO PUBLISHING LIMITED

Introduction

The gap between starting to learn an instrument and playing 'real' music is a very great deterrent to many players. Consequently, I, and some other composers got together to tackle this problem.

We are producing a series of pieces for many different instruments, playable by musicians with limited technical ability. As a guide, each has a grading similar to those of the Associated Board of the Royal Schools of Music, but I hope people of all grades will enjoy playing them.

Richard Rodney Bennett

Richard Rodney Bennett
Series Editor

Summer Music

FOR FLUTE AND PIANO   Richard Rodney Bennett

Flute

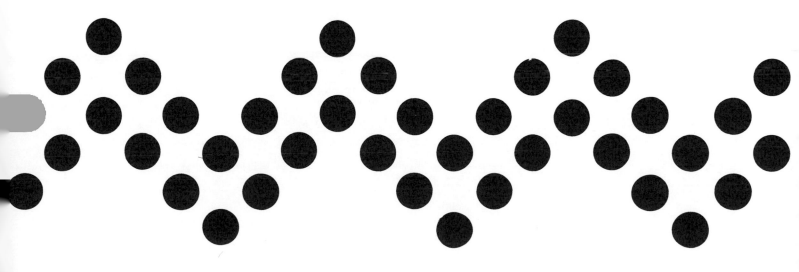

Order No: NOV 120560

NOVELLO PUBLISHING LIMITED

FLUTE

for Angela and Chris

SUMMER MUSIC

RICHARD RODNEY BENNETT

2 SIESTA

3 GAMES

6

sempre con molto moto

poco cresc.

mf

f

poco dim.   mf

dim.   p

cresc. poco a poco

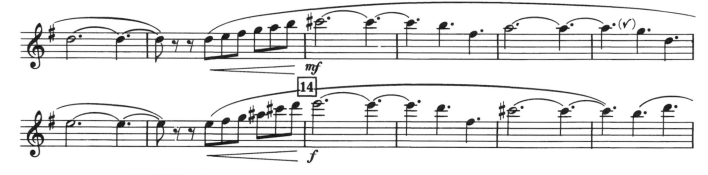

f giocoso

ff al fine

sff

NOVELLO
PUBLISHING LIMITED
14-15 Berners Street, London W1T 3LJ
Exclusive Distributors:
Hal Leonard Europe Limited Distribution Centre
Newmarket Road, Bury St Edmunds, Suffolk IP33 3YB

Order No: NOV 120560

for Angela and Chris

SUMMER MUSIC

RICHARD RODNEY BENNETT

1

4

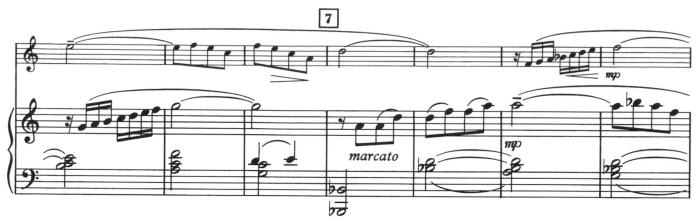

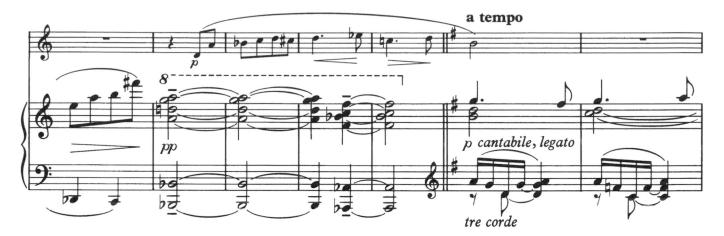

a tempo

l'istesso tempo ma tranquillo

una corda

pochiss. rall.

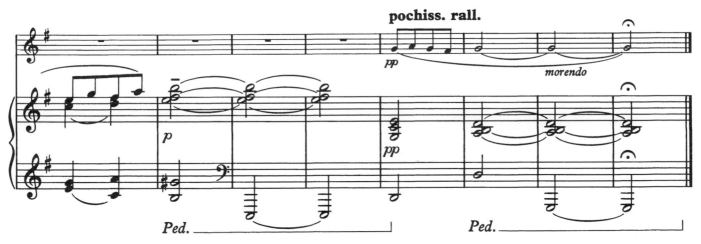

Ped.⎯⎯⎯⎯⎯⎯⎯⎯⎯⎯   Ped.⎯⎯⎯⎯⎯⎯⎯⎯⎯⎯

2 SIESTA

Lento e dolce ♩ = 58

p espress.

p

con Ped. una corda

p espress.

Ped. ⌐⌐⌐⌐ simile
tre corde

mp

mp

p

poco cresc.

poco cresc.

mf

mf

Ped._____ con Ped.

4 pochiss. più mosso

legato

Ped. _____ Ped. simile

non solo

5

più marcato

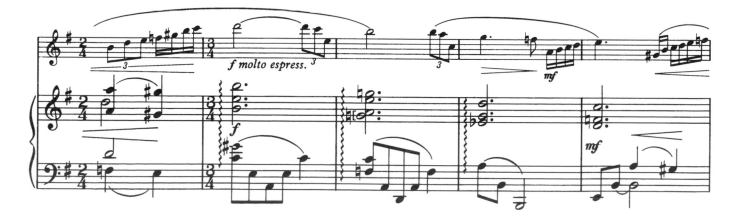

f molto espress.

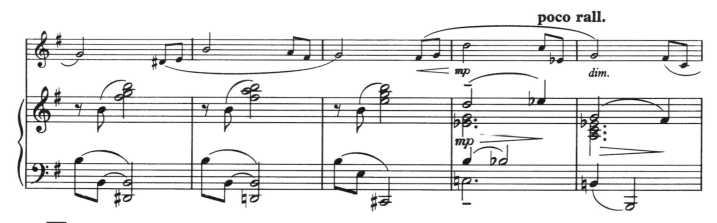

3 GAMES

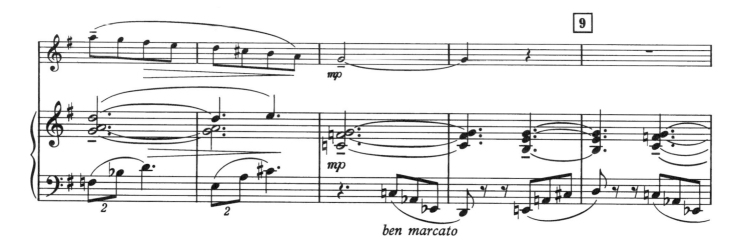

sempre con molto moto

sempre con Ped.

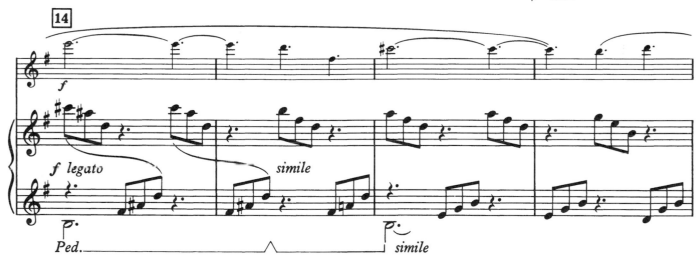

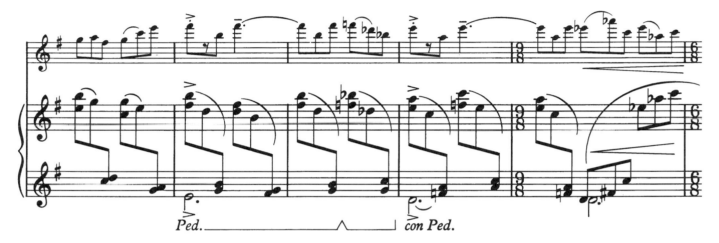

TREVOR WYE

VIDEO

PLAY THE FLUTE
A beginner's guide

TUTORS

A BEGINNER'S BOOK FOR THE FLUTE
Part 1
Part 2
Piano Accompaniment

PRACTICE BOOKS FOR THE FLUTE
VOLUME 1 Tone
VOLUME 2 Technique
VOLUME 3 Articulation
VOLUME 4 Intonation and Vibrato
VOLUME 5 Breathing and Scales
VOLUME 6 Advanced Practice

A PICCOLO PRACTICE BOOK

PROPER FLUTE PLAYING

ARRANGEMENTS FOR FLUTE & PIANO

A COUPERIN ALBUM
AN ELGAR FLUTE ALBUM
A FAURE FLUTE ALBUM
A RAMEAU ALBUM
A SATIE FLUTE ALBUM
A SCHUMANN FLUTE ALBUM
A VIVALDI ALBUM

A FIRST LATIN-AMERICAN FLUTE ALBUM
A SECOND LATIN-AMERICAN FLUTE ALBUM

MOZART FLUTE CONCERTO IN G K.313
MOZART FLUTE CONCERTO IN D K.314 AND ANDANTE IN C K.315

SCHUBERT THEME AND VARIATIONS D 935 No. 3

Novello

611 (90)